THE LITTLE BOOK OF CARTY

Compiled by Dave Murray

Illustrated by Kirk Walters

Toledo Blade Company

541 North Superior St.
Toledo, Ohio, 43660

Tel: 419-724-6069
Fax: 419-724-6191
E-mail: **dmurray@theblade.com**
Web site: **toledoblade.com**

First published in the United States in 2008

Copyright@2008, by The Blade

ISBN: 0-9770681-4-5
ISBN13: 978-0-9770681-4-2

All rights reserved; no part of this publication may be reproduced, stored in a retrieval system, or transmitted in any form or by any means, electronic, mechanical, photocopying, recording, or otherwise without the prior written permission of the Publisher. This book may not be lent, resold, hired out, or otherwise disposed of by way of trade in any form of binding or cover other than that in which it is published without the prior written consent of the Publisher.

Printed and bound in the United States by University Lithoprinters, Ann Arbor, Michigan.

This book is printed on acid-free paper.

FOREWORD

Carleton S. Finkbeiner, just Carty to everyone in Toledo, Ohio, is a once-in-a-generation politician. Instantly recognizable by sight or first name only, everyone seems to have a "Carty story," something they remember that their mercurial mayor has said or done.

Toledo's cheerleader-in-chief, Carty is the city's most enthusiastic backer, whether in or out of the mayor's office. Almost his entire career has been spent serving the people of Toledo.

In his three terms as mayor, Carty traveled the world to extol Toledo's virtues, to tell business and political leaders from Europe to Asia what a fine place Toledo is to live and work. His hard work paid off in numerous awards for Toledo, which was named under his mayorship an All-American City and a Most Liveable City and just this year received the "America in Bloom" award.

You see, Carty loves flowers and has had them planted along city streets, in the middle of city streets, and in parks across the city. Toledo has bloomed under his benevolent leadership.

He led the drive for Toledo to keep its beloved Jeep plant, he gave up his own condo along the Maumee River to make way for a new Owens Corning world headquarters, and he introduced Toledo to Scout, his golden Lab whose presence at city hall seems to keep everyone's mood just a little lighter — especially Carty's.

Along the way, Carty and his antics, eccentricities, and the vicissitudes of his mayoral reign gave us all a few precious moments of laughter, or for the lowly city worker who dared not move fast enough or showed up a few minutes late for a staff meeting, more than a few moments of pain.

That simply may be why Toledoans continue to return Carty to the mayor's office time and time again. After all, what would we do without Carty Finkbeiner to lead us, inspire us, make us laugh, and make some of us cry?

This small book, this chronicle of Carty if you will, was inspired by a similar volume penned last year about London's colorful mayor, Boris Johnson.

The Little Book of Carty is dedicated to Carty, whose heart knows no bounds for its love of Toledo but whose mouth sometimes gets in the way.

— *Dave Murray, The Blade*

IN CARTY'S
OWN WORDS

Turbulence:
Carty and the deaf

"I think there may be people out there interested in living in a nice home if the noise factor was not going to be a problem."

November, 1994, Carty promoted the idea that deaf people could be moved into homes around Toledo's airport after a new air cargo hub spawned scores of noise complaints. "That's like saying let the blind work at night because they can't see," said Dave Wielinski, chairman of Barrier Free Toledo. The idea landed Carty in the 1997 humor book *The 176 Stupidest Things Ever Done.*

Crash landing:

Carty sheds a tear

"I would ask us to tame some of the savageness. No, I would ask us to tame a lot of the savageness."

November, 1994, Carty broke down in tears at an emotional press conference after his deaf-living-at-the-airport comments earned him national ridicule, insisting he didn't mean to be insensitive. But by the end of the news conference, he said he would still pursue the idea. "All we wished to do was to have the opportunity to sit down and talk and see if there is any interest whatsoever," he told reporters.

Carty's pursuit of the idea, despite protests from the deaf community, prompted an immediate response from the Ability Center of Greater Toledo, which issued a statement saying it was disappointed that Carty "failed to accept responsibility for his comments, to acknowledge their inappropriateness, and to apologize for the comments."

Demographic breakdown:

Carty on water, suburban sprawl, and minorities

Expansion of Toledo's water system outside the city is "largely responsible" for suburban sprawl, in addition to "the concern for living next to poor, sometimes homeless, hungry minorities in the city."

July, 1995, Carty explained the steady loss of Toledo's population in his weekly radio address. In a speech before the Oregon-Northwood Area Chamber of Commerce a few days later about Toledo's policy of selling water to its suburbs, Carty expanded on his philosophy of minorities and where they like to live, saying that Jewish people tend to want to live near their fellow Jews. He then added: "White people tend to live where there is a majority of white people. Black people feel more comfortable living where there's a majority of black people." He added that minorities increasingly choose to live in cities and as a result, "social-economically, minorities are not as advanced" and their standard of living is not as high.

Following publication of his remarks, Carty, in an "open letter to the citizens of our community," apologized for his comments: "I was emphasizing the importance of selling water at a fair price to benefit all the citizens of Toledo now and in the future."

The day he released his letter of apology, Carty became testy with a reporter. He referred to himself as a "damned good mayor" and said, "Maybe I'll give you a wimp, and then you'll see what the city looks like."

Painting the town:

Carty's official color scheme

"I think we need some consistency and coordination in our color scheme."

August, 1995, Carty announced "Toledo teal," "Glass City gray," and "Frogtown brown" as the city's official colors as part of his Brighten Toledo beautification campaign. The colors were used in city painting projects from bridge rails to utility poles.

Fowl play:

Carty and chickens

"I've told you once. I'm not going to tell you again. You have to get rid of the chickens."

July, 1997, Carty telephoned Toledo resident Christy Szych, who applied for a city permit to keep her two pet chickens — named Original and Extra Crispy — at her home. Ms. Szych was given the two fuzzy chicks as a graduation gift and as they grew had kept them in her backyard in a 12-foot-by-5-foot pen. She dutifully applied to the city for a permit to keep them legal, but on a Sunday, Carty called to tell Ms. Szych that he would not allow chickens in the city.

"They didn't really cause any trouble. They were just like dogs to me. They came when you called them. They walked on leashes," Ms. Szych said.

City officials told her they would view her request more favorably if her neighbors would sign a petition supporting her application. All of her neighbors agreed to sign the petition, but Carty got wind of her request. He "got very, very mad at me," she told a reporter. She took her pets to a farm outside the city but said she would get her revenge on the mayor: "He lost my vote."

Short-sheeted:

Carty and the KKK

"They'll probably have about 4,000, maybe 5,000, for the finals, and it will look like they're conducting some sort of a mini-version of a Ku Klux Klan meeting in a corner of Gund Arena."

January, 1999, Carty was not pleased when the Mid-American Conference announced that it would pull its men's basketball tournament from Toledo and move it to Cleveland's Gund Arena. He was trying to explain his views on a WSPD-AM morning radio show when he came up with the KKK analogy.

Carty later explained that he meant nothing racial by the reference. He said he was attempting to make a joke about the likelihood of low turnout when he remembered a scene from a rerun of an *All in the Family* episode in

which Archie Bunker mistakenly went to a sparsely attended Klan rally in a large arena.

The KKK was not pleased with Carty, issuing a statement: "The Ku Klux Klan, perhaps one of the most detested political organizations in the history of the United States of America, has issued an official statement denying all knowledge of Toledo Mayor Carty Finkbeiner." And local Grand Dragon Bud Brennings declared, "Carty Finkbeiner is not a Klansman. We would not allow such a hateful man in our ranks."

Slap shot:

Carty, hockey, and pizza

"I'm gonna buy homemade and seasoned pizzas!"

March, 1999, Carty called a press conference and told Toledoans to boycott Little Caesars Pizza because its owner, the Ilitch family of Detroit, was supporting development of a suburban sports arena to compete against the Toledo Sports Arena and the Toledo Storm hockey team.

The Ilitches, who also own the Detroit Red Wings and the Detroit Tigers, had just signed a deal to move the Red Wings' top minor league affiliate to a $48 million arena being built in Rossford (the project was later abandoned).

The day after Carty called for the pizza boycott, defenders of the little guy in the toga fired back. Little Caesars franchises in Toledo changed the name of their popular Crazy Bread to Carty Bread, and one location offered a "Carty Special" — a $5 large ham pizza. Little Caesars' sales skyrocketed. "We've got more than 100 calls today from people supporting us," said one store owner.

Call of the wild:

Carty and his frogs

"Can you imagine what would've happened if those frogs drowned? It's bad enough people think I beat up my employees and throw them out the 22nd-floor windows. I can't let them think I'm taking my anger out on innocent frogs, too."

March, 2001, Carty explained his quick action to verify the safety of two frogs donated to the mayor's office to commemorate "It's Reigning Frogs," a downtown frog art display. City Law Director Barbara Herring noticed the frogs didn't have a rock to sit on and were coming to the surface of the water to get air.

"I'm worried about those frogs," she told the mayor at a staff meeting. "I'm worried, too," Carty said. He picked up the conference-room telephone. "Get me the Toledo Zoo reptile department!" he told the operator. "This is Mayor Carty Frogbeiner!" he barked to the zookeeper. "We have two frogs who may need your help!"

Within the hour, herpetologist Greg Lipps swept into the room, a load of reference books tucked under his arms. A quick examination showed they were African clawed frogs, genus xenopus. They were amphibians, not reptiles, and fully aquatic, he said. The two young frogs were in no danger of drowning — but once they grew, they could jump out of the tank and shrivel up on the mayor's waiting room floor.

City staffers quickly sealed possible getaway routes. Life returned to normal at Government Center.

Ready to rumble:
Carty the brawler

"I'd be delighted to meet you sometime — just you and I. I'd be delighted."

August, 2001, Carty challenged Herbie Howard to a fight over the condition of his Old Orchard gas station after the two took turns jabbing their fingers in each other's faces. "You're challenging me to a fistfight?" Mr. Howard shouted as Carty turned and walked away into a crowd which had gathered after Carty called a press conference at Mr. Howard's business.

Slippery situation:

Carty's lube job

"I was not screaming. I was louder than normal."

June, 2003, Carty's life between stints as mayor was still a bit tense, with his temper occasionally flaring up. Police were called to the ProCare Automotive Service Center on Secor Road one morning after Carty blew up at Sandra Crawford, a ProCare employee who offered him a free oil change because the job took a little longer than expected. She told police that Carty "was screaming and using profanity" when he came for his car and it was not yet ready.

"I felt she was a little indifferent to the problem. She was trying to make the problem go away by saying, 'You don't have to pay for it,'" Carty told a reporter after the incident became public. "If my name was Carty Smith, I don't believe any phone call would have been made, any report to police. That is not an excuse. I accept the challenge to myself in terms of communicating better."

21

Dog day afternoon:
Carty and Scout

"Hi, I'm Mayor Carty Finkbeiner, and this is my good friend Scout. I want to tell you something that I learned recently: On a hot day, do not leave your dog in the car."

September, 2007, Carty made a public service announcement for the Toledo Humane Society after he was given a $100 ticket for parking his city SUV in a handicapped space and leaving his yellow Labrador retriever in the vehicle for 45 minutes on a hot day. He said he parked in the handicapped space because it was shaded and rolled the windows down but later agreed to do the public service announcement to warn pet owners of the dangers of leaving pets in vehicles on hot days.

Filmed sitting on a bench along the Maumee River with his dog, Carty looked at Scout and told him, "On the next hot day, you're stayin' home, Scout!" Then turning to the camera, Carty said: "Play it cool with your pets. Don't risk your pet's life! Leave them at home!"

Gas pains:
Carty and World War III

"If Columbia Gas goes to a temporary headquarters and/ or permanent headquarters anywhere but Toledo, World War III will erupt in Columbus and Toledo."

December, 2007, Carty didn't respond well to the news that Columbia Gas of Ohio planned to move its headquarters temporarily from downtown Toledo. The declaration of war worked. The company stayed put.

CARTY
ON THE JOB

Holding pattern:
Carty and the dispatcher

"My name is Carty Finkbeiner and I'm a city councilman … Sir, right now your ass is in trouble and if you don't give me your name you'll be in more trouble. I don't like your attitude one damned bit."

April, 1980, Carty called Toledo police about a citizen complaint, but the call turned sour when dispatcher John Munk had to put Carty on hold when an accident call came in. When the dispatcher came back on the line, he tried to soothe the irate councilman, telling him, "I voted for you in the last City Council election." That didn't work. "I don't give a damn if you voted for me," Carty told Mr. Munk.

Silence ... or else!

Carty consults with others

> "You just shut up. I don't want to hear anything out of you or I'll smash your face."

November, 1990, Councilman Carty erupted at city Human Resources Director Bill Logie during a meeting with Mayor John McHugh and top city administrators to discuss the status of labor negotiations. Mr. Logie later said the tirade continued "with Carty sticking his finger in my face."

Mayor McHugh apologized for the outburst, saying he would "talk" to Carty.

Office space:

Carty's secretary

"I cannot walk on water. I am like a whipped puppy now."

April, 1994, Carolyn Wiley, in tears, quit after two weeks on the job as Carty's administrative assistant, saying she could no longer endure his constant criticism. She said the final straw came when Carty berated her over a typo she had made after working 12-hour days while being criticized daily.

"Here I am, 59 years old, unemployed, and I am my sole supporter," Ms. Wiley said after she quit. "What bothered me the most was that he made me feel like I was not qualified, but I know I am. I told him I would not be demoralized anymore."

Enough already!

Carty's law director

"I simply could not tolerate another temper tantrum by the mayor against members of my staff."

July, 1994, City Law Director John Mattimoe had enough, resigning from his $74,000-a-year post after another of his employees felt the lash of the mayor's temper. Carty chewed out a city lawyer for not keeping him informed about the sale of the mayor's Middleground condominium, at a $128,000 profit, to make way for the new Owens Corning headquarters downtown.

Carty said following the resignation that he was "very angry" at the law department for not keeping him informed about the condo sale negotiations. "I think it's safe to say I took him to the woodshed. I was very, very angry."

Not-so-positive reinforcement

Carty's pep talks

"Some mornings he'd come in and chew our asses up and down because we weren't strong enough."

August, 1994, Ron Jackson, one of Carty's top aides, retired after more than three decades of city service as a police officer, deputy police chief, and executive director of the Board of Community Relations. "The long hours, the stress — it's just not conducive to someone in my condition," said Mr. Jackson, who suffered from high blood pressure. "I need sufficient rest and a stable schedule. Anyone who knows the 22nd floor knows you won't get that up here that often."

Mean streets:

Carty the paver

"There was ample opportunity to get on the contractors and demand from them that if they wanted to get paid on a timely basis, they had to complete their work on a timely basis."

November, 1995, Carty's goal of repaving 30 miles of city streets was going to fall short by three miles, so the mayor docked the pay of Ray Norris, city transportation commissioner, $1,000 for every mile not paved. Poor weather had hampered paving crews that summer, but Carty said it was his policy to reward city workers for good work and punish them when they didn't measure up. In fact, the mayor gave Mr. Norris a $5,000 pay raise earlier in the year before cutting his salary $3,000.

Strange brew:

Carty and the coffee mug

"We are just like Monica Lewinsky and President Clinton — she stroked him for so long, then he threw her to the wind."

November, 1999, Carolyn Smithers, manager of the Erie Street Market, recounted Carty's words during a tense encounter. Ms. Smithers knew Carty wasn't happy with her work, but she wasn't prepared for what he told her in a meeting at city hall.

After his Monica Lewinsky comparison, Carty had another piece of mayoral advice for Ms. Smithers: "Be a man — don't be a girl." She had heard enough and got up to leave the meeting. That's when he "swung his arm with the coffee mug in it up to the side of my face" striking her in the head.

Ms. Smithers sued, and after two years of legal wrangling, City Council voted to give her $35,000 to settle out of court.

And in this corner ...

Carty and the chest bump

"He's not going to put his finger in my face or threaten me, and that's that."

January, 1999, Councilman Bob McCloskey had heard enough. What began as a mayoral finger wag in the face in a city hall conference room ended in the two rising and obscenities flying, with the councilman bumping chests with the mayor and shoving him away. "It's a manhood issue for the mayor. I think he needs psychiatric help," Mr. McCloskey said.

The two were discussing Carty's plan to move a city office to a park in Councilman McCloskey's district, a proposal the councilman objected to. Mr. McCloskey

said after the altercation that he had "a very heated discussion" with Carty. "It could have been a lot worse than it was" if Carty had responded, the councilman said.

Carty didn't want to talk with reporters after the incident but said: "I did not get out of hand except to present my position quite vigorously."

Lodging a complaint:
Carty in secret shopper mode

"I don't want our city to be seen as an unclean city."

May, 2007, Carty addressed a press conference in front of the Hotel SeaGate after personally delivering to hotel manager Shannon Fielder a scathing report about the conditions found by a secret shopper hired by the mayor to surveil the hotel.

"We do get complaints. They think we're dirty, but we're not. We're very clean. We're just old and outdated," Ms. Fielder said, before turning the tables on Carty, saying her guests complain about the lack of activity in Toledo's downtown.

"They constantly complain of nowhere to shop, nowhere to walk. They walk out front of our hotel and see Fort Industry Square, which is 90 percent empty. We defend the city constantly."

What People Say About Carty

Game, set, match!

Carty and the volleyball spat

"He started yelling at me. He took an intimidating swipe at me … He just got ugly, nasty."

April, 1996, J. Robert Roemer, local volleyball club owner, bid farewell to Carty's downtown volleyball venture. The mayor's grand plans for volleyball players to compete at the city's new, $250,000 sand volleyball complex in International Park hadn't worked out. The lack of lights for night play, a liquor license, and a fence to keep balls from rolling into the river had kept players away, and Carty was not pleased.

Mr. Roemer, owner of La Jolla Beach Volleyball Club, agreed to run the courts for the city the first year but walked away from the job before the second season began after he said Carty took an open-handed swing at him, grazing his nose. "You just don't treat people that way if you want to make things happen," Mr. Roemer said. "The mayor has no clue what a business is about. He talks about entrepreneurs, but he doesn't know what an entrepreneur does."

Kind words:

Carty the "dynamic man"

"The mayor had a significant impact on my career, and I will always be grateful. The mayor is a dynamic man, and I think I'm a better person to have worked this closely with him."

June, 1996, Chief of Staff John Alexander, the last of Carty's original inner circle, announced his resignation, telling reporters, "This is an amicable parting." Carty said Mr. Alexander was leaving his post because concerns about his health caused him to seek a "less-pressurized" atmosphere.

City councilmen groaned when they learned of Mr. Alexander's resignation "to pursue other interests in the public or private sector" but said they had expected the mayor's overworked, right-hand man eventually to burn out. "If you looked at John you could see how drawn out and frustrated he was. Nobody, but nobody, can keep up with Carty," said Councilman Bob McCloskey.

Gritting and not bearing it:

Carty tunes out

Carty "slammed the rear passenger door into her, knocking her to the pavement," the police report stated, adding that his teeth were "gritted and veins popping out" when he hit her with the door.

September, 1996, WSPD-Radio reporter Tricia Taylor tumbled to the ground while trying to interview Carty as he opened his car door at the end of an hour-long press conference about the city's tax-abatement program. Observers reported seeing the reporter fall to the ground after Ms. Taylor followed Carty to his car.

She filed a criminal complaint against Carty telling police she was asking the mayor questions about recent staff turnover in his office while standing next to his car when he slammed the car door into her. She was treated at Toledo Hospital.

Seven weeks earlier, WSPD asked Carty to refrain from touching Ms. Taylor after she complained that he put his hand on the back of her shoulder as they walked through a doorway at a reception for Toledo Public Schools' superintendent candidates.

After WSPD's request, Carty said Ms. Taylor was acting rude and hounding him for an interview. The mayor said he was walking with the reporter into a hallway when he put his hand on the back of her shoulder to guide her through the door before him.

Driven to succeed:

Carty loves Toledo

"I would say he probably reinvented the city of Toledo. There's nobody that loves the city any more. There's nobody that works any harder than Carty does. He drives his people the same way."

May, 1997, Sandy Isenberg, president of the Lucas County Board of Commissioners, described Carty's devotion to Toledo. "We have differences of opinion. We're both very strong-minded people," but Carty has done an excellent job as mayor. "He has had the opportunity to do a lot of things for the city of Toledo. He has worked very hard."

Busted!

Carty the cop

"I don't get it — like he doesn't have something better to do."

May, 1997, motorist Richard Weber admitted he "rolled through" a red light on the rain-slickened Anthony Wayne Trail after trying to stop at Copland Boulevard. Fortunately, no one was driving through the intersection, but unfortunately for Mr. Weber, Toledo's mayor witnessed his traffic infraction.

Carty wasn't going to let Mr. Weber slide by, taking off after him. At the next intersection, at Detroit Avenue, Carty used his car to block Mr. Weber's car, gave him a lecture, and later signed a "citizen's complaint" charging him with running a red light.

"I am still shaking," Mr. Weber said two weeks later. "God knows I didn't do it on purpose. I apologized to him and said I did not mean to slide through the intersection. I tried to explain. He didn't want to listen."

A local judge threw out the complaint, saying the mayor didn't use the proper form.

Spousal support:

Amy defends Carty

"I wish people could see the real Carty, the one I know and love. He cares for Toledo in ways most people never see."

October, 1997, Amy Finkbeiner, Carty's wife, offered support for her husband in a TV ad designed to soften his image during the 1997 race for mayor. He was re-elected.

Your time is up!

Carty the parking enforcer

"He lectured me on morality. He told me that the church needed to be more concerned with the moral issues of parking."

March, 1998, the Rev. Gary Bell, pastor of Park Church, encountered Carty as the mayor wrote notes to drivers of vehicles parked along Harvard Boulevard.

Pastor Bell showed the mayor a sign allowing members of his nearby church to park on the boulevard on Sundays, but the mayor wasn't in the mood for ecclesiastical excuses.

"You'll have to move it," Carty told Pastor Bell, whose own vehicle was receiving a hand-written mayoral parking ticket. "I pointed to the sign over the mayor's shoulder. It says, 'No Parking Any Time Except Sundays.' The mayor confessed then that he didn't know there were any signs up," the good pastor said. But Carty kept writing tickets.

"I explained to him the parking problems that city churches face, that Park Church members have been

parking here for 80 years, but the mayor said he just doesn't agree," Pastor Bell said. "When he found out who I was, he made it clear he didn't care what I had to say. His opinion was what mattered."

While Carty didn't use foul language or take the Lord's name in vain, the cleric said, he did say the parking matter was an ethical issue. "He lectured me on morality. He told me that the church needed to be more concerned with the moral issues of parking. I told him he didn't need to lecture me about morality."

Power play:

Carty the dictator

"I have never experienced anyone on our police department who has exhibited such a blatant disregard for the profession of law enforcement and most importantly the Constitution of the United States."

August, 1998, D. Michael Collins, president of the Toledo Patrolman's Association, wrote to Carty, telling him that he was acting like a "wacko dictator from some banana republic." Carty drew the ire of the Toledo police union and the ACLU after he ordered Police Chief Mike Navarre to rid the city of drug dealers living on Oakwood Avenue. "This is a property with problem citizens.

Harass, intervene with, do what is necessary to clean out these folks."

"The mayor's statement is reprehensible, probably illegal ... This mayor has, over time, demonstrated a disregard for the fundamental protections of citizens," said Chris Link, executive director of the ACLU.

Too close for comfort:

Carty and the great-grandmother

"He listens a little, screams a lot, calls you degrading names, and moves closer and closer until he is inches away from your face, saliva flying."

October, 1998, Joann Vanderpool, a longtime community and Democratic Party activist, received a profanity-laced tongue lashing from Carty in a city parking garage after she expressed support for the construction of a Rite Aid drugstore in her South Toledo neighborhood. The mayor, who opposed the store, used God's name in vain repeatedly, the great-grandmother wrote in a letter of protest to City Council. "Over and over again, I was either 'stupid' or 'crazy' and it began with 'God damn.'"

Councilman Bob McCloskey, who represented Ms. Vanderpool, said Carty had gone too far: "To talk to her that way and to cuss at her, it's just uncalled for. There is something wrong with the man's mind to talk to a lady that way. I think he needs psychiatric care."

Potty mouth:

Carty and the bar of soap

"Is there a mayor in the United States who expresses his public temper as if he is playing pool badly in a bar? If so, please identify your peer."

December, 1998, consumer advocate Ralph Nader had a bar of soap delivered to the mayor's office after Carty called a press conference to say that a story in The Blade about the expanding government costs to build a new Jeep plant in Toledo should have been "shit-canned."

"There is a feature of your coarse verbosity that is fairly consistent over time," Mr. Nader wrote in a letter to Carty. "You direct your sneering, barnyard language away from corporate executives and their corporations and focus on the people you were elected to serve."

And the soap? "A cleaner tongue may induce a cleaner mind — at least that is the aspiration behind the gift," Mr. Nader told Carty.

Sympathy gesture:
Carty's graffiti

"It's a quiet neighborhood. I think it's unfair; Carty cares so much about Toledo."

July, 2000, mayoral neighbor Joan Gordon expressed her support for Carty as she walked her dog past his South Toledo driveway the morning after vandals struck. In white paint they wrote on his driveway: "Government blows. Authority overruled." The graffiti artists also drew a large phallic symbol next to their message.

A shock to the system:

Carty and the restaurateur

"The attack was so sudden, so unexpected, and so intense it just terrified the old man."

July, 2000, Toledo lawyer John Potts described how his client, restaurant owner John Skiadas, was treated by Carty during an encounter at the Erie Street Market.

The mayor berated Mr. Skiadas over delays in opening Pepe's Mexican Restaurant & Cantina, a new eatery at the market that the city was helping to finance — leading to an angina attack and hospitalization of Mr. Skiadas within hours of the confrontation. "Carty was yelling at him, throwing threats at him. He said he would make trouble for him and close him down. He said he would get health inspectors to throw him out of Toledo," Maria Skiadas said after her father's hospitalization.

Paul Garza, a Toledo businessman who witnessed Carty's tirade, said the mayor appeared to be in a rage and almost seemed as if he was not aware of how he was behaving and could not control it. "The mayor was vicious, and he seemed to enjoy it," Mr. Garza said.

Off target?

Carty's management style

"Council and city administrators alike are constantly scrambling to fix problems created by your 'READY-FIRE-AIM' management style."

September, 2000, City Council President Peter Ujvagi responded to Carty's criticism that council failed to act on a proposed ban on assault weapons for the city. Mr. Ujvagi said council does not drag its feet but takes time to carefully study and often repair the legislation forwarded to council by the administration.

Mad frog malady:
Carty's disease

"Carty suffers from mad frog disease. There are three symptoms. One is, you act like a toad when you should be acting like a prince. Two, you're an egomaniac. And the third is, you think the lily pad you're on is the focus of the universe, rather than worrying about the health of the pond."

June, 2001, Steve Serchuk, chairman of the Toledo-Lucas County Plan Commission, had just learned that a commission staff member was sent back to Toledo by Carty from the Detroit airport because the mayor wanted the staffer's boss, Steve Herwat, to accompany him on a trip to brief Census Bureau officials about Toledo population numbers.

Carty penalized Mr. Herwat for trying to send a subordinate on the trip by ordering Mr. Herwat "not to come up to the 22nd floor for the duration of the mayor's tenure, and he is not to attend the staff meetings," punishment that surely earned Mr. Herwat his colleagues' envy.

So much more than silliness:

Carty as a "great mayor"

"The day will come when we think about who moved Toledo ahead, who saved [Owens Corning], who saved Jeep, who moved to beautify the city, who brought housing to the near-downtown area.
He did all that."

November, 2001, Mayor-elect Jack Ford said history will remember Carty as "one of our great mayors." Acts that earned Carty notoriety — "silly things," Mr. Ford said — were "part and parcel of Carty's style."

A whole lotta bull:
Carty's pasture

"To use his words, he is 'the big bull in the pasture.' If he decides he wants to be the only bull in the pasture, I'll find another pasture."

June, 2006, Toledo Police Chief Jack Smith had enough and resigned following a heated discussion with Carty about how to deal with gang problems in the city. "Carty is not a coach. He is not a cheerleader. He's a senior executive of a major city, and he needs to act like that." The chief said the confrontation "was very close to being physical" and that an administrator stepped between him and the mayor.

Carty tried to downplay the incident. "If anybody here thinks this 67-year-old man is going to take on a stronger, younger ex-Marine with a revolver on his hip, you're wrong," the mayor said during a press conference after the dust-up with the chief.

War games:

Carty and the U.S. Marines

"Carty feels it is OK for Marines to die in Iraq, but just don't come to Toledo."

February, 2008, former U.S. Marine Brian Thompson, 40, of West Toledo, said he was in disbelief when he picked up The Blade and read that Carty had kicked the Marines out of downtown, where they had come to train in urban warfare in a vacant building. "The better trained the men and women are, the better chances that they'll come home alive," Mr. Thompson said.

Carty said he did not want a repeat of the last time the Marines trained downtown, in May, 2006. "I saw the military with guns drawn emulating warfare, and I observed the expressions of citizens. There was a look of wonderment on some people's faces, and there was a look of fear on other people's faces."

One man's opinion:
Carty and the voice-mail hacker

"Carty Finkbeiner is a complete moron."

February, 2008, an unknown hacker decided to register a complaint against Carty by changing the telephone voice-mail greeting for the city's purchasing hot line. The unofficial greeting was changed as soon as the mayor's office was informed about it to: "Thank you for calling Toledo, the most liveable city."

THE CARTY FILE

Name: Carleton See Finkbeiner, Jr.

Age: 69

Address: Townley Road, Toledo.

Marital Status: Married twice, currently to the former Amy Wittman. His first wife, the former Valerie Jan Lavin, was Miss Ohio in 1965.

Children: Two daughters by his first marriage, Jenny and Katie.

Occupation: Mayor of the city of Toledo. In fact, Carty was elected in 1993 as the city's first strong mayor in modern times after voters did away with the weak mayor-city manager form of government. He is now serving his third term as mayor. After his first two terms, from 1994 to 2001, he sat out a term and won re-election to a third term in 2005. By city charter, he could run for another four-year term as mayor in 2009 before being required to sit out again. There is no age limit for mayor in the city charter.

Political affiliation: Currently a Democrat, but Carty has run for elected office as a Republican, independent Democrat, and leader of his own independent political party — Citizens Organized and United for a New Toledo.

Loves: Besides his wife, daughters, and five grandchildren, and of course Toledo, Carty loves University of Michigan football, where he was once offered and turned down an assistant coaching job; he still has season football tickets. On the eve of new Wolverine Coach Rich Rodriguez's first practice this year, Carty personally delivered to his home a sheet cake with the words "Good luck Rich. Go Blue!"

A LITTLE
BIOGRAPHY
OF CARTY

A former writer for The Blade, John Nichols, probably summed up Carty best in 1985 when he wrote: "In many senses, Carty Finkbeiner's political odyssey reminds one of the line from an old song by the Grateful Dead: 'What a long, strange trip it's been.'"

Carty came of age politically in the turbulent 1960s, not as a radical anti-war protester, but as a "Democrat for Nixon" in 1968. That is before he became a "Republican for McGovern" in 1972.

In between, in 1969, was an event that first brought Carty to the attention of the public, but as almost always, his moment of triumph was quickly tarnished by his own actions.

As an up-and-coming 30-year-old with a good education from an established Perrysburg family, Carleton See Finkbeiner, Jr., was named "Young Man of the Year" by Toledo's Junior Chamber of Commerce in 1969.

A few eyebrows were raised with his nomination for the annual honor. As a Jaycee board member, he headed the program to make the selection but resigned the post after he was nominated by his pastor at St. Paul's Episcopal Church in Maumee and named one of 10 finalists.

Within a day of receiving the award came the news that Carty was unemployed, although the papers nominating him, as well as the award dinner program, stated he was the administrative assistant to the regional supervisor of the Ohio Department of Urban Affairs.

Jack Branum, Toledo regional supervisor for the urban affairs department at that time, told the press that Carty did not work for him, had never worked for him, and was not scheduled to work for him. And Albert Giles, state urban affairs director, said: "There is no such job. I don't know where Mr. Finkbeiner got that title from."

As the controversy swirled, Carty told a reporter that he hoped to obtain a government job through his connections with Republican

Gov. James A. Rhodes, who was the main speaker at the Young Man of the Year award dinner, but he admitted he did not have the job when he supplied information for his nomination.

Within a week, Carty relinquished the award and gave back the trophy he had received. As a precursor to his political career to come, the brouhaha generated six stories in The Blade, a letter to the editor, television and radio coverage, and the threat of a lawsuit if he didn't return the award.

The job controversy was one that would dog him when he later ran for elected office, with critics leveling the charge that he had never held "a real job."

But that was unfair. In fact, Carty held numerous jobs, just not for very long.

After graduating from Maumee Valley Country Day School in 1957 — where he was president of his freshman, sophomore, junior, and senior classes and quarterback of the football team — he attended Trinity College in Hartford, Conn., for two years, but because of a football injury and homesickness, he returned to Ohio and graduated from Denison University in 1962, where he majored in speech and communications.

After college, Carty accepted a position as a sixth-grade teacher and assistant football coach at Maumee Valley.

In early 1963, he decided he liked coaching football and applied and was interviewed for assistant coaching positions at the University of Minnesota and the University of Michigan, which offered him a job.

But before he took the job at Michigan, he interviewed with newly hired Toledo University football coach Frank Lauterbur, who offered him a coaching position as well. In 1963, he became a graduate assistant football coach at Toledo for $1,200 a year plus room and board. The next year he was hired as a full-time assistant at $7,000 a year, a job he held through the 1966 season.

He left TU, now the University of Toledo, saying he had become disenchanted with coaching and was considering a career in the

THE LITTLE BOOK OF CARTY

ministry or business.

In April, 1967, he hired on as a trainee at the former Bell & Beckwith stock brokerage but resigned within three months, telling a partner at the firm that he lacked the motivation to pursue a brokerage career.

Carty then decided to enter the ministry and was interviewed for admittance to an Episcopal seminary near Washington, but because he could not begin his studies immediately, as he had hoped, he decided against entering the seminary.

While in Washington, Carty made a simple but fateful decision to visit with Toledo's congressman at the time, Thomas "Lud" Ashley. He later told a reporter that as he gazed upon the lighted Capitol dome that evening, he was struck by its majesty and began to dream of being elected to Congress.

When Carty returned to Toledo, the congressman's brother, Charles Ashley, a trustee of the Economic Opportunity Planning Association, which funded urban renewal and anti-poverty programs in the city, helped him land a job as an assistant director of the East Toledo Neighborhood Opportunity Center.

Carty was quickly promoted to employment coordinator and then associate director for urban affairs, but as with his past jobs, he just as quickly became "fed up" with the work and with the people in charge of the agency he worked for.

In a letter to his boss at the time, the legendary EOPA Director Wayman Palmer, Carty wrote: "Where is your integrity, where are your guts?" concluding that Mr. Palmer was "hung up on Mickey Mouse junk" and was doing nothing for Toledo's poor. Carty also wrote in the letter that he was entitled to a raise.

In a letter of reply, Mr. Palmer wrote that he resented the assertion Carty had aided relations between the black community and Mr. Palmer, who was black: "Your assumed role of the Great White Savior is not appreciated ... Have you ever been a team player or do you always feel a psychic need to be a quarterback? Impetuosity has always retarded your total growth."

A few months later, in 1969, Carty left the agency after he was accused of shouting and swearing at people. Another EOPA director, John Jones, said Carty got in fistfights while working in the neighborhoods and came to work scarred from the encounters.

Carty then went through a string of jobs, from census taker, to a sportscaster for WSPD-TV, to a salesman for New England Mutual Life Insurance Co., where he sold $1.3 million in policies in a year, winning recognition as one of the firm's top agents in the United States.

He then became director of conferences at Bowling Green State University, where two people who worked with him described "childlike" temper tantrums, swearing, and false accusations.

Finally, Carty turned to his dream of a career in politics, a dream that had awakened in him that night in Washington several years before after visiting with Congressman Ashley. His target? The same Mr. Ashley whose brother got Carty his first job in government.

It was 1974, and instead of working his way up from the precinct level, Carty set his sights on the top locally elected office — a seat in the United States House of Representatives.

Despite being a Republican for McGovern two years before, he had no problem landing the Republican nomination to challenge Congressman Ashley. It was an improbable contest. Congressman Ashley had won 70 percent of the vote in 1972, and Carty was a political unknown.

But Carty surprised everyone by almost winning. He lost to one of the most influential Democrats in Congress in a heavily Democratic district by fewer than 7,000 votes out of 140,000 cast. It was the closest anyone had come to unseating Mr. Ashley since he was first elected to Congress in 1954.

Despite the loss, Carty didn't stop campaigning, taking on Congressman Ashley again in 1976. But this time Mr. Ashley had learned his lesson. He ran hard, raised more money, and spent more time back home in Toledo. He beat Carty by 17,000 votes the second time around.

Carty then set his sights a bit lower, running and winning a seat on Toledo City Council in 1979. But before his first term was over, he decided once again he was destined for higher office, running in 1981 for mayor against incumbent Democrat Doug DeGood.

Carty campaigned hard on the problems facing the city, but a week before the election, attention focused on an incident during one of his more novel campaign practices — handing out leaflets in traffic.

One of the drivers in a three-car pileup at Secor Road and Monroe Street blamed Carty for stopping traffic at the busy intersection. Press coverage of the crash was relentless, and after several days, Carty called a press conference to complain. He blamed The Blade and criticized the newspaper for endorsing Mayor DeGood for re-election, saying editors supported mediocrity.

He then did the unthinkable for a politician — he broke down and wept in the midst of the press conference.

For local political pundits, who remembered the devastating effect crying had on the 1972 presidential campaign of Democratic Sen. Edmund Muskie, Carty's tears were the end of his mayoral hopes. But instead, Carty's popularity only increased.

He lost to Mayor DeGood by only 1,800 votes, the closest Toledo mayoral election up to that time. Carty the Republican won the majority of Democratic wards in the city, running especially well in black and white working-class neighborhoods, while Democrat DeGood eked out victory by winning in the wealthier Republican wards, which had higher voter turnout.

Carty learned from his defeat and decided to set off on a different path again, this time helping to form a new political organization — Citizens Organized and United for a New Toledo, COUNT for short, a grass-roots political party that fielded two candidates in the 1983 City Council race.

COUNT candidate Carty Finkbeiner won, placing third in the race for eight seats and becoming the first independent elected to council since 1959.

Soon after the election, COUNT faded away, and by 1985, Carty registered as a Democrat and screened for a Democratic Party endorsement for council. But Democrats didn't want him.

That didn't stop Carty from running again — this time alone.

He showed up at campaign events without the aides who shadowed other candidates; he marched in the Labor Day parade with local construction unions instead of riding at the head of the parade with the other politicians.

Carty was a tireless campaigner.

"He'd be there when I came in at 11 at night and when I got done at 7 in the morning, just shaking everybody's hand," said one local hospital worker.

On the eve of the election, when other candidates headed home to bed, Carty was still hitting the bowling alleys, all alone, wearing a jogging suit, shaking hands, and greeting many people by name.

The few television campaign spots Carty could afford highlighted his lack of party support: "I have no party ... I have only you, the people," he said, looking into the camera.

The strategy worked. He came in a strong second among the eight City Council winners.

After winning council seats as a Republican, an independent, and an independent Democrat, and losing a mayoral race running as a Republican, Carty decided to run as a Democrat for mayor in 1987, this time against a popular Republican incumbent — Donna Owens.

He lost again, and was forced to sit out another two-year term, but was returned to council by voters in 1989 and 1991.

In 1992, Carty began campaigning again, this time not for himself but to change the city charter. He led the successful effort to change Toledo from a city-manager to a strong-mayor form of government.

That goal achieved, he ran for mayor for a third time in 1993, beating Councilman Mike Ferner by a razor-thin margin of 672 votes out of 92,000 cast.

With greater power and authority than any Toledo mayor in decades, and blessed with a strong national and local economy, Carty in his first term was able to build hundreds of new houses in the inner-city, open the Erie Street Market, and turn the shuttered Portside Marketplace into COSI, a science museum that drew families from throughout the region.

Yet for all his initial mayoral triumphs, his football-like intensity caused numerous top Toledo officials to flee city service, saying they were tired of being yelled at, browbeaten, and treated like first-half losers.

Four months after Carty became mayor, his administrative assistant, through tears, told reporters that she felt like a "whipped puppy" and resigned. A half dozen city administrators would later blame Carty's temper tantrums for their departures.

For a time, a hole in the scale model of downtown Toledo in the mayor's office gave witness to his short fuse. Staff members said he slammed his fist into the model in a fit of rage when two administrators failed to show up at a staff meeting.

Bill Boyle, a former city councilman and harsh critic of the mayor, told reporters at the time that Carty was "a two-faced guy."

"He has a very outgoing way about him. He slaps people on the back and shakes hands. But behind the scenes, he treats people like dirt," Mr. Boyle said.

Carty defended his management of what he called "Team Toledo."

"I set goals for this team and I expect people to meet them," he said in 1997 as he was running for re-election. "I expect hard work. I expect the very best."

Down in the polls, Carty fought hard and won a second four-year term as Toledo's strong mayor.

Carty's second term as Toledo's first modern strong mayor was even noisier.

There were calls to boycott pizza, offers to fight a gas station owner, mayoral parking tickets issued on a Sunday morning to a local congregation, and His Honor's decision to chase down and ticket a motorist he saw roll through a red light.

And he continued to treat his top managers like third-string bench warmers.

Carty banished the city's real estate manager, who was a few minutes late to a weekly staff meeting, to sit for hours alone in an isolated conference room. The manager quit a few months later.

He tried to fire a top mayoral assistant who was diagnosed with cancer. The assistant opted for sick leave and sued the mayor. The city paid him $132,500 to drop the suit.

And then there was the mayoral coffee cup to the side of the head of the manager of the Erie Street Market, whose performance was not up to Carty's standards. The city paid $35,000 to make that lawsuit go away.

We'll call all that the dark side of Carty, or "the bad Carty" as Blade editorial writers have labeled him. The "good Carty" can be very good for Toledo.

He's been a road-paving maniac while in office, on the backs of city engineers and street managers to lay down as much asphalt as possible each summer. The pay of a Team Toledo transportation manager was cut $1,000 for every mile Carty wanted paved but wasn't before the snow flew.

Carty led the effort to keep Jeep in Toledo, which resulted in the construction of a $2 billion factory complex in North Toledo, and convinced Owens Corning to build a new $100 million world headquarters on the banks of the Maumee River downtown. And after the recession of the early 1990s ended with downtown on its knees, with more buildings empty than full, Carty almost single-handedly breathed life — with the help of taxpayer dollars — into the empty Commodore Perry and Hillcrest hotels and the former LaSalle department store. He also backed the Mud Hens moving from suburban Maumee to a new downtown ballpark (Fifth Third Field).

Even out of office after his second term he continued to fight for Toledoans in his "It's Just Not Right" segments for WTVG-TV Channel 13, keeping his face before voters and raising ratings at the ABC affiliate.

And after four years with Jack Ford at the helm, voters in 2005 overwhelmingly embraced Carty for a third four-year term as their mayor, even with the news that he had survived a heart attack.

He told a live television audience two weeks before the election that he stayed fit by healthy eating, regular exercise, and "never losing my temper," he pledged. "Well," he then added, "two out of three isn't bad."

Moving back into the city's top office as a trimmer, older, and, many said, wiser mayor, Carty supported the building of a new $100 million hockey arena downtown and pushed the redevelopment of the riverfront in East Toledo, but "the bad Carty" rears his head every now and then.

He ordered the U.S. Marines to leave downtown after they had set up for a weekend of urban warfare training, and Jack Smith quit as police chief after a heated confrontation with Carty.

"To use his words, he is the big bull in the pasture. If he decides he wants to be the only bull in the pasture, I'll find another pasture," Chief Smith told the press.

But no matter what Carty has said or done over the years, he is strong for Toledo, as the song goes, and has made it his life's work to see the city grow and prosper, even if a few butts have to be kicked at city hall or a few citizens chased down and reminded to obey the traffic laws.

Through it all, Carty has remained steadfast in his belief that the citizens of Toledo are what count most.

"There are two kinds of politicians: those who put their heart and soul into their jobs and have the courage to do what they need to do without fear of what other people will think and those who don't," Carty once told a reporter.

Hail to the Victors, Carty. You've outmuscled, outhustled, and outlasted the best of them.

— *Dave Murray*

THE LITTLE BOOK OF CARTY

Compiled by Dave Murray

Illustrated by Kirk Walters

Edited and designed by Douglas Koerner

Copy edited by Todd Wetzler

Special thanks to the numerous Blade reporters who had the fortune or misfortune of covering Carty Finkbeiner throughout his long career in Toledo politics. And special thanks to Blade editorial librarians Vesna Radivojevic and Jordie Henry for the hours it took to pull from The Blade's morgue all the crazy things Carty said and did over the past four decades.

Photo of Carty on Page 82 by Amy E. Voigt